A puppy can be playful, but it can also be a handful! It is a big decision to become a dog owner. You must be sure that you will be able to take care of a dog for its whole life, not just when it is a cute baby. Many breeds grow to be big and strong!

# Dalmatian

This dog breed has a white coat with black or brown spots. The spots only appear when the puppies are a few weeks old. It is common for a mother to have six to nine puppies at once.

Dalmatians have lots of energy and can keep running for miles.

Dalmatians often have poor hearing or are deaf.

# American Staffordshire Terrier

Lively, clever, and bright-eyed, these dogs grow to a medium size. They have a short coat in all sorts of patterns and shades.

This breed is friendly and makes a loyal family dog.

Watch out if you take this dog for a walk. They like to lick people! They are also strong enough to pull you along.

# Saint Bernard

This breed is one of the largest, heaviest dog breeds. However, they are kind, gentle, patient pets. Unfortunately, adult Saint Bernard dogs are also muddy, messy, and drool a lot!

A Saint Bernard's thick coat is great in winter. In summer it can make the dog overheat, so give your pet somewhere cool to rest.

Saint Bernard puppies love to chew things. Keep your toys and socks out of the way!

# Labrador

This breed often has golden fur, but is also seen in black and shades of brown. It is one of the most popular breeds to keep as a family pet. The puppies are lively, but calm down as they get older.

These dogs are clever and kind. They are often trained to help people or to compete in dog shows.

Labradors are the most popular breed of pet dog in the US and the UK.

# German Shepherd

This is one of the cleverest dog breeds. They can be trained as police dogs, rescue dogs, and to help people who have a disability. They can open doors, push buttons, and even use a washing machine!

A well-bred German shepherd dog has pointed ears that stand upright.

Keep your German shepherd fit and healthy with two walks a day.

# Beagle

Most dogs have a much better sense of smell than a person does. A beagle's nose is especially sensitive. Beagles love to follow an interesting scent through the park!

Beagles can be noisy dogs. They bark, but they also make a howling noise like a wolf.

A beagle adores
eating! Keep all
of your food out
of reach behind
closed doors.

Boxer dogs are well-known for their goofiness and energy. They love to jump and play and have fun. They often run round and round, chasing their own tail.

Some boxer dogs have their tail clipped short, or docked, when they are a puppy.

Boxer dogs have a very short, smooth, and shiny coat.

# Pug

The pug is the clown of the dog world! They are tiny but energetic, and love to show off. Many people love them for their flat face and cute black nose.

Most pugs have pale fawn fur and a short, curly tail.

A pug's squashed nose can make it hard for it to breathe in hot weather.

# Springer Spaniel

Bouncy and energetic, these hunting dogs need a lot of exercise. They have soft, silky ears, a waggy tail, and a gentle, adoring look on their face.

Springer spaniels bark a lot if a stranger comes to your house.

Keep your spaniel close to you around water. They love to swim!

# Yorkshire Terrier

Many terriers are small, but Yorkshire terriers are tiny! They are popular show dogs with their dark eyes and long, glossy coat. It needs brushing, nearly every day if possible.

These dogs have a mixture of black and tan fur. It can be clipped short or left long and parted in the middle.

The breed's nickname is Yorkie. Some owners choose them because they lose less fur than many dogs.

# English Bulldog

Cute bulldog puppies grow into medium sized, square adults. They have wrinkles on their forehead, droopy cheeks, and a pushed in nose.

They are kind, patient dogs. They also love to snooze a lot!

Bulldogs have big, square jaws. Their bottom teeth stick out farther than their top teeth.

# Poodle

These curly-haired dogs are bred in different sizes. Miniature and toy poodles are the smallest, and standard poodles are larger.

Poodles are clever and friendly. They get lonely if left alone for too long.

A poodle's fur is thick as well as curly. It is often clipped short on some parts of the body.

# Rottweiler

A Rottweiler puppy is a small, cute, bundle of fun. They grow into large, strong dogs that need good training.

Rottweilers need exercise and company. If you leave them for too long they may chew and destroy things.

A sleeping Rottweiler can snore very loudly!

# Great Dane

The Great Dane is one of the tallest of all the dog breeds. Its head can be as high as a person's chest.

Their great height allows them to reach food from any table or worktop. Keep it out of sight!

Great Danes have an extremely large, long head with floppy ears.

# Dachshund

These dogs are very easy to recognize. They have short legs and a long, barrel-shaped body. Their head is neat and small, with a pointed snout.

They may be little, but Dachshunds have a very big bark!

Dachshunds like to poke their snout into your business, whether you are fastening your shoes or trying to do a puzzle.